I0493053

QUAIL FARMING FOR BEGINNERS

A Quick A To Z Beginners' Guide On
Raising Healthy Quails

Copyright © 2016

All rights reserved. No part of this publication may be reproduced, stored in a retrieval system, or transmitted in any form or by any means –electronic, mechanical, photocopy, recording, or any other – except for brief quotations in print or online reviews, without the prior permission of the author.

While the author has made every effort to ensure the information contained herein is accurate and up-to-date, you are encouraged to read this book alongside other books covering the subject matter. No amount of knowledge or information is ever enough. Keep searching for more.

Dedication

So much valuable information on raising quails has been covered in this book. Significantly, the contents herein are intended for those wishing to raise quails for the very first time. I therefore, dedicate it to every beginner quail farmer.

Acknowledgements

To the many people who offered their invaluable views, ideas and support towards the writing of this book, I am humbled. In particular, let me thank all the members of my family, friends and relatives for their relentless prayers and support. May the Almighty God bless you abundantly!
Finally, but most important, I thank God for the gift of life and for His endless blessings upon my life. Indeed, great is His faithfulness. His grace, love and mercy endure forever!

Table Of Contents

STARTING QUAIL FARMING AS A BEGINNER

Quail birds are flock animals. They thrive best as a group.

In the poultry farming industry, raising quails has today positioned itself as one of the most lucrative undertakings. It can be started with little capital, and has high returns on investment. But most significant, you need to raise quails in the right way in order to cut wasting money on birds that die or birds that don't lay eggs.

Below are the initial steps you need to take to help you embark on the lucrative journey of raising quails as a beginner.

Get relevant exposure – Visit some of the already established quail farms within your locality and learn firsthand from the owners how they take care of the birds. Even if it means paying some small fee to get access to such farms, never hesitate to do so. Aim to get their invaluable practical advise on keeping quails to enable you get a clear picture of what you want to get into.

Have enough capital – Truth is, you will need limited capital to successfully start quail farming. This is unlike keeping other poultry breeds which may require more capital to begin. Notably, the large chunk of money you will use in quail farming will go towards purchasing the birds and the birds' essentials like feeds and housing.

Capital may also be handy to help you get a good location for keeping the birds in case you don't have an adequate space at your backyard.

Be licensed – This is next step towards starting a successful quill farm. I guess you would not want to play hide and seek game with the authorities. Due to their endangered nature, most governments across the world insist on those intending to raise quails to first get relevant approvals/licenses. They also do this to help curb spread of diseases like bird flu and other poultry related diseases which may be spread quails. However, there are certain countries where it is not necessary to be licensed to start keeping the birds. Ensure you get the license if you reside in a country where acquiring it is a pre-requisite to raising the birds.

Choose a good location – A number of small scale quail bird farmers prefer raising the birds within their backyards. If you have limited capital but have adequate space at your backyard, you can adopt keeping the birds at the backyard. But if you have enough capital, you can rent a big space and build a spacious structure to house the birds. However, whatever system of rearing you decide to settle on, remember, the birds must be taken good care of.

Choose a location which will not be an inconvenience to you and your neighbors. Equally, the location must be free from predators and noise since quails are usually unproductive in unsafe and noisy environments.

Get good quail breeds – Depending on your production purpose, choose good quail breeds that will adequately serve that purpose. There are different quail breeds. Some are good in egg production while others are known good broilers. If you are embarking on quail farming for purposes of egg production, you need to choose good egg layers. But if you want to raise quails for meat production, you will need to get good broilers. How far you will go in your quail farming venture will be hinged on the quality of quail breeds chose to keep.

An overview of the general care needed by quails – The quality of outputs from quails is always directly proportional to the breed of quails you are keeping and the quality of care they are given. Their house must be well ventilated and kept clean at all times to improve on their productivity and help curb spread of any disease. And when building their house/cage, ensure you leave spaces enough to prevent the birds from escaping. If left in the open, the birds can easily escape and disappear.

Equally, you need to expose layers to adequate amount of sunlight, or artificial light (in the absence of sunlight). They are more productive if exposed to light for longer duration of hours (12 to 14 hours a day).

Still, you need to feed them on well balanced diet. And most vital, provide them with fresh and clean water placed at strategic points where they do not need to strain to access it.

COMPONENTS OF A GOOD QUAIL FARMING BUSINESS PLAN

Making any business plan is never enough. You must follow it religiously to breathe life into it.

Although many people embark on keeping quails without a quail farming business plan, I would strongly suggest you start with one. A quail farming business plan will guide you towards running a sustainable and profitable venture. As noted earlier, if you are starting quail farming for the very first time, you need to visit some local quail farms and witness firsthand how the birds are taken care of. Visiting the farms will expose you to all the pros and cons of keeping the birds and best-prepare you for the journey a head.

When drafting a quail farming business plan, you need to capture the below with clarity:

Your purpose of production – Why do you want to keep the birds? Do you intend to keep them for commercial gains or for meeting your home consumption needs of fresh eggs and meat? Or do you simply want to raise them for fun/as a hobby? You need to clearly define your purpose of raising the birds.

Products to produce – Before deciding on the products to produce, you need to carry out an extensive research on the bird's products that are on demand and may offer you value when you finally embark on producing them. Generally, there are four major areas you can settle on:

- Raising the birds for egg production.
- Raising the birds for meat production.
- Raising the birds for both eggs and meat production.
- Breeding – Selling of fertilized eggs, day old quail chicks, a week old quail chicks, two weeks old quail chicks…etc.

Housing – Quails need a safe and secure housing with all necessary facilities provided to guarantee their safety and healthy growth. This would in return motivate them to stay productive. They can be raised in either cages or on floors. But you must ensure that their housing is properly ventilated and that the birds are given well balanced feeds and fresh water for drinking. The subject of housing is clearly detailed further in this book.

Labour – If you have a larger quail farm or you may be too pre-occupied to tend to the quails, you can employ services of laborer to help you. Notably, quail birds are usually very easy to manage and as a result, you will be required to rely on minimal extra labour.

Feeds – The quality of the products you will derive out of your birds will depend on the quality of feeds you give them. Since quail birds are fussy feeders, ensure you provide them with well balanced feeds, placed at proper positions where they do not need to strain to access them.

Did you know an adult quail bird can consume a maximum of 30grams of feeds a day? But the feeds need to have sufficient amounts of proteins in them since the birds need the proteins for production of eggs and to maintain their feathers.

Quail birds can comfortably feed on chicken or turkey feeds. They equally consume fewer feeds as compared to other breeds of poultry. As a result, feeding them would attract lesser capital investment as compared to feeding other poultry breeds. The subject of feeding quails is also further detailed in this book.

Breeding – Male quails are generally very active and can comfortably take good care of at least 5 females a day. However, for purposes of breeding, it's advisable to keep the males and females in a ratio of 1:3 (one male for every three females).
Since domesticated female quails are poor egg hatchers, you need to find a good egg incubator to help you hatch their eggs; if you chose to keep the birds for breeding purposes.

Proper Care – Quails are known to be resistant to a number of diseases affecting other poultry birds. However, they are prone to infections which may arise out of poor care and poor management. If you take good care of the birds, you will be shielding them from health-related issues.

Marketing – To be able to profitably gain from quail farming venture, you will need a good marketing strategy which will allow you to sell the produced products at competitive prices. And to help you set good prices, you need to know your total cost of production so as to ensure that your total selling price is always higher than your total cost of production.

Some of the ways of selling quail products include: supplying eggs in crates to local grocery stores and supermarkets. Selling via internet through use of social media like Face book and Twitter. Going to the local agricultural shows and selling the products to the attendees.

Note: Other than selling the eggs in trays, you can too process, package and brand quail meat and sell to local groceries and supermarkets

QUAIL EGGS

Female quails begin to lay small-sized multicolored eggs at the age of 6 weeks. They can lay an average of 25 eggs in a good month, translating to over 300 eggs in a good year (especially the female Japanese quails)

I believe you've already had a glimpse into what awaits in the quail farming adventure. Let's therefore get into details.

There are several ways of starting quail farming, but the two most common ones are either starting with hatching fertile quail eggs into chicks through incubation, or getting live birds (preferably quail chicks) from breeders or local quail farmers. It is therefore vital to understand how to identify good quail eggs suitable for incubation, and to go through the incubation process. Afterwards, we shall go through taking care of quail chicks into adulthood (from the brooder into cages/aviaries).

How to identify a quail egg unsuitable for incubation

If you are getting quail eggs for the first time for purposes of incubation, it is vital to be able to tell if the eggs are fertile and suitable for incubation. This is necessary to help curb cases of incubating abnormal and unfertilized eggs which would lead to massive losses of resources and time.

Before presenting quail eggs for incubation, it can be a tough task for an average quail farmer to tell a normal and fertile quail egg from an abnormal/infertile one. Generally, it would be heart-wrenching to incubate infertile quail eggs and wait for them to hatch.

Below are some of the four observable abnormalities which can render a quail egg unsuitable for incubation.

- Cracks on the eggshell.

- Absence of an egg yolk / presence of double yolk.
- Soft eggshells / very thin eggshells.
- Very dark spots/blood spots/bloody ring around/in the yolk. (These can be detected through candling).

How to verify the fertility of incubated quail eggs

The first step towards ensuring an egg laid by a quail bird is fertile is through correct pairing of the birds: one male to a maximum of three females. On the seventh day of incubation, you can candle the eggs again to establish their fertility. Using a candling lamp, a fertile egg will exhibit a reddish embryo while an infertile one will show a clear embryo. But if you aren't sure about the colors on the seventh day, you can again candle the eggs on the 13th or 14th day of incubation. If the chick is absent, you will observe a larger section of the egg containing a clear embryo with minimal space left for air, but if the chick is present, the embryo will appear darker in color, or the light may not be able to penetrate through the eggshell.

Note: Take lots of precaution when candling quail eggs since they have a delicate eggshell. Avoid candling them against devices with strong/hot flames.

INCUBATION

For an incubator to hatch quail eggs, it has to provide suitable temperature, relative humidity, and adequate fresh air. Equally, you should religiously turn the eggs with a 180°, three times in 24 hours (to ensure uniform heating), except during the last three days to hatching (day 15 and onwards).

How to successfully incubate quail eggs

Quail eggs take an average of 18 to 24 days to hatch. However, there are emerging mutants of quails whose eggs may take an average of between 14 to 17 days to hatch.

From my own experience, the hatching rate of quail eggs is usually high for eggs presented for incubation seven or eight days and below from the day they are laid. Eggs older than eight days have a lower hatching rate. Significantly, eggs older than ten days have a lower rate of hatching.

To guarantee a high hatch rate, use eggs seven days old and below. The incubator should be properly cleaned and disinfected, and the temperatures inside the incubator should range between 37.5^0c (99.5F) to 38^0c (100.5F). (Always remember to read the manufacturer's manual on how best to handle the incubator).

You should put the eggs at room temperature for a few hours before putting them inside the incubator. Ensure they are clean, fresh and free from abnormalities (you can candle them to check this out).

Always remember, for an incubator to hatch quail eggs, it has to provide suitable temperature, relative humidity, and adequate fresh air. Equally, if the incubator is a manual one, you should religiously turn the eggs with a 180^0, three times in 24 hours (to ensure uniform heating); except during the last three days to hatching (day 15 and onwards).

Next, we shall take a look at some of the leading causes of poor egg-hatch and solutions for each cause.

Below are the **six leading causes of poor egg hatch and solutions for each case.**

- **Incubating infertile eggs:** It can truly be a painful ordeal to stay optimistic in wait for chicks to hatch from infertile quail eggs! In fact it would be regarded as a miracle should the infertile eggs hatch!

  Solution: You should candle the eggs before and during incubation (before the 15th day) to help detect infertile eggs. But prior to that, you should correctly pair the males vs. the females to guarantee fertility of the eggs laid by female quails.

- **Incubating defective/abnormal eggs:** An egg may be regarded to be with a defect if: it has cracks on its outer shell, its shell is contaminated, has the presence of a double egg yolk or absence of the yolk, has very dark spots or blood spots or bloody ring around or in its yolk.

  Solution: Candle the eggs prior to incubation to ensure abnormal eggs do not see the inside of an incubator. You need too to collect eggs laid by female quails regularly (at least two times a day) and store them in a humid room with pointed ends facing downwards.

- **Failure to turn incubated eggs:** The main reason for turning eggs during incubation is to guarantee uniform warming of the eggs. Failure to do so may result into overheating of one part/one side of an egg thus rendering it unsuitable for hatching chicks.

  Solution: During incubation, commit to turning the eggs at least three times every twenty four hours. Equally, you can use an automatic egg incubator with a proven ability to turn eggs at the required angel of 180^0, three times in 24 hours.

- **Lack of favorable conditions inside the incubator**: As already noted, for a fertile quail egg to be effectively hatched, the incubator has to provide: suitable temperatures, relative humidity and adequate fresh air.

  Solution: Use egg incubators with proven ability to hatch eggs. Equally, you need to clean and disinfect the incubator before use. And if you reside in an area which experiences several power failures, have a power back up to guarantee smooth functioning of the incubator (in the absence of electric power supply).

- **The eggs may appear fertile when candled but still fail to hatch chicks:** This could be a result of incubating eggs from older quail breeds. Equally, it could be an effect of incubating eggs which have taken too long after being laid.

  Solution: Always incubate eggs from younger and mature breeds of quails. Equally, incubate eggs which are utmost 7-8 days old and below. Desist from holding laid eggs for longer than 8 days in the storage facility as this may greatly lower their rate of hatching.

  Do not attempt to wash any dirty egg with water. Doing so may block the natural egg's protective layer and expose it to entry by organisms, thus hamper its ability to hatch chicks.

  And before placing the eggs in an incubator, ensure they are first stored at room temperature.

- **Poor management of the egg incubator.** Poor control of temperatures and humidity inside the incubator can be disastrous to egg hatching. Unclean and poorly disinfected incubator/hatcher may too contribute to poor egg hatching.

  Solution: Ensure the incubator has the right and consistent temperatures and humidity throughout the incubation period. Have the incubator placed inside of a room where no change in temperature and humidity can easily occur. Equally, take time to clean and disinfect the incubator before using it.

TAKING CARE OF QUAIL CHICKS
All the basic essentials every good brooder should have

Quail chicks take an average of 18-24 days to hatch from a successfully incubated egg. When the chicks are hatched, they usually have an attachment of egg yolk in their lower body (abdomen). Do not scrap this yolk away since they need it as a source of food for the first few days (two days) as they acclimatize with their new way of life.

Do not be sacred at the size of quail chicks. They are usually tiny, but have the ability to feed on their own. On the other hand, the chicks are delicate and sensitive to cold and hot temperatures. To prevent the chicks from drowning in water troughs, you should half-fill the water troughs with small-sized marbles.

There are two ways of acquiring quail chicks: getting them from reputable quail breeders, or through successful incubation of fertile quail eggs. The chicks are afterwards transferred to a brooder and below are some of the basic essentials which should be present inside any good brooder.

Source of heat: This is necessary to help heat or regulate the temperature inside the brooder. Sources of heat may be in form of electric bulbs, gas burners or charcoal burners.

The brooder should be correctly heated. The two best ways to verify this is by use of a thermometer and, or by closely observing the behavior, movements or positions of the chicks around the heating source. In case they tend to crowd around the heating source, that's a sure sign of presence of cold in the incubator. But if they are hiding at the walls of the incubator (far away from the heating source), that's a sign for too much heat in the brooder. When the brooder is correctly heated, the chicks should be evenly spread and will be seen to be normally going about their business.

The temperature inside the brooder should be maintained at 95F during the first week. Afterwards, it should be lowered by at least 5F on each passing week until the 4th week when the birds should be ready to be taken out of the brooder. Gradually, you should withdraw the source of heat by the fourth week to allow the birds adapt to the surrounding environment.

Litter: The main function of litter is to aid in keeping the brooder warm by absorbing wet moisture. The litter may be in form of sawdust or wood shavings. Already used litter should be immediately discarded from the brooder to avoid spillage of any undesired odor from the brooder to the surrounding.

Waterers: The waterers should be constructed in such a way the chicks cannot step or defecate on them. At all times, the drinking water should be made available in plenty. It should be clean, fresh and placed at convenient locations to avoid stressing the birds.

Half-fill the waterers with marbles to bar the chicks from drowning in them. One of the leading causes of early mortality of quail chicks is drowning in the waterers.

Don't forget to have the waterers cleaned promptly before filling up (you should clean them on a daily basis). And after two to three weeks, you can remove the marbles from the drinking water.

Feeders: Just like waterers, clean and adequate feeders should be placed at convenient locations where chicks do not need to strain to access them. The feeders too, should be constructed in such a way the chicks cannot step or defecate on them.

Well balanced feeds rich in proteins should be made available to the chicks at all times. As a good recommendation, you can feed them on game bird feeds /turkey feeds (a starter with an average protein component of 25%).

Once the birds attain the age of four weeks, you should prepare to change their feeds to layers mash. Since quails start laying eggs at 6 weeks old, you should change the feeds to layers mash as the birds approach that egg laying stage.

Adequate ventilation: There should be adequate circulation of fresh air in the brooder. This is vital to allow for gaseous exchange and to keep respiratory-related infections at bay.

Correct amount of light: The brooder should be correctly lit to allow the chicks see the feeds and water. For small scale operations, the heating bulb can as well serve the purpose of lighting the brooder. You can use infrared heating bulb in a brooder housing quail chicks eight days old and below. It will both serve as a source of heat and light. Interestingly, infrared bulbs will not interfere with the sleeping patterns of the chicks inside the brooder.

Note: The brooder should be located at an ideal location away from noise and disturbance. It should securely protect the birds from predators. And most significant, you need to exercise good grooming when handling quail chicks. They should be raised under sanitary conditions.

TIPS ON GETTING SUITABLE INITIAL QUAIL BREED

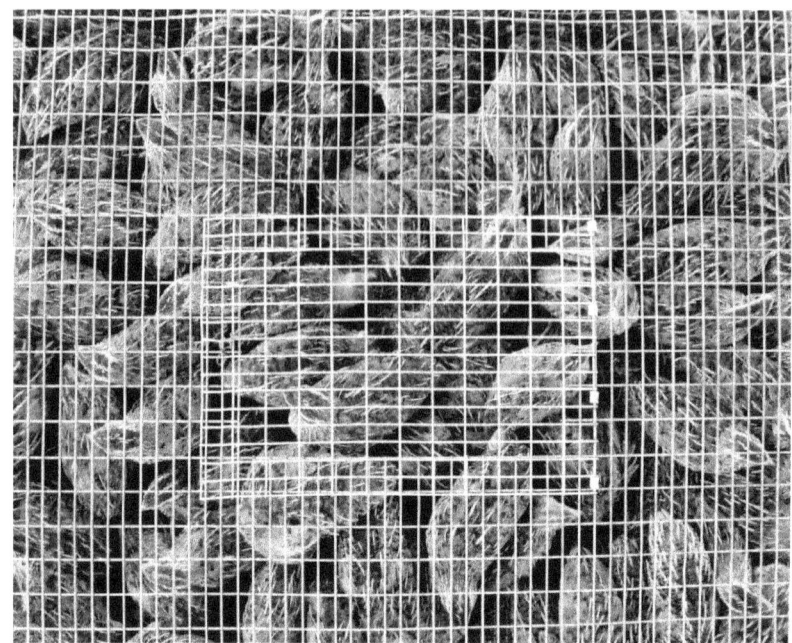

If you start with a desirable breed, you should expect a desirable output. But if you start with an undesirable breed, you should expect an undesirable output. **It's that simple!**

The best breed of quail bird to keep is largely dependent on your purpose of keeping the bird. World over, people keep different quail breeds for different reasons: for provision of fresh eggs, for provision of meat, for provision of both eggs and meat, as domestic pets, for commercial gains…etc.

Did you know different quail breeds have different personalities? Before settling on any quail breed to keep, you need to do enough research on your need for keeping the bird, and the type of personality you would want your quail to exhibit. Afterwards, visit a few established quail bird farmers or quail breeders within your locality to have that invaluable firsthand experience on the behavior and production capability of your desired quail breed.

Significantly, for starters, the best breed of quail bird to raise should be locally and readily available. The type quail breed you start out with will determine the quality of gains from your quail farming venture. Therefore, you need to be extra keen when selecting your initial flock of quail breeds.

The following six tips should help you make a good decision when getting your first flock of quails to raise.

- Visit at least three different local quail farmers to witness their purpose of raising the quails, the quail breeds they are keeping and the production capabilities of the quail breeds.
- Are there licensed and reputable quail breeders or quail dealer outlets within your region? These are the people/places you should give first preference when you decide to buy your first flock of quails. Aim to acquire the best performing breeds available from them.
- Avoid purchase of breeding flock with deformities or those of different sizes and different colors. They will most probably not get along (they will always be fighting) resulting into low, unprofitable outputs.
- Stick to one type of quail breed. Avoid mixing different quail breeds as they may not be friendly to one another, especially if they are being raised in the same cages.
- Establish the history of mortality or diseases of the breed you intend to purchase. Most breeders or dealers have these records in their possessions.
- If you decide to purchase quail eggs for incubation, insist on getting eggs with equal (similar) sizes, shapes and colors. Equally, buy eggs with no abnormality.

QUAIL SEXING

How to differentiate a female quail from a male quail

How can you tell that a quail bird is male or female?

If you intend to raise quails for either egg or meat production, you must be able to differentiate a female quail from a male one. It would be painful to raise male quails and expect them to lay eggs sooner or later. Or to raise female quails and expect them not to lay eggs.

Below are four most common ways any beginner in quail farming can use to identify whether a quail is male or female.

- **By examining the physical appearance:** On attaining maturity, female quails appear bigger in size than male quails of the same age and breed.

- **Examining quail's vent/cloacae:** This is one of the most effective ways of distinguishing a male quail from a female quail. There are two ways of examining the vent. First, when you press the area around it with your two fingers, a small ball-like lump may pop forward suggesting the bird is male. If the ball-like lump fails to show up, then that would signify the bird is female. Also, when you press the vent, you may see presence of some white foam coming out of it, suggesting the bird is male. The absence of that foam may signify the bird is female.

- **Roosting of the birds:** At five weeks, several male quails begin to roost (they begin to make some soft sound/noise). You can therefore, rely on the roosting to help you tell a male quail from a female quail. It's the male birds that roost.

- **By checking the color pattern on quails' chests:** Female quails have speckled feathers on their chests while male quails have plain feathered chests. However, this method is only applicable on quails which have already grown enough feathers; usually at three weeks old and onwards. It is also effective to use on quails with speckled feathers like the Cortunix.

KEEPING QUAILS FOR PROFIT
(Commercial Quail Farming)

Today, it is no longer a secret that compared to other poultry birds, raising quails require less capital investment but offers great returns.

Many beginner quail farmers always wonder whether keeping the birds can really be profitable! Well, truth is, quail farming can either be a heaven or a nightmare depending on your approach. If you start with the right birds, the right housing unit, the right environment, correct feeds and clean water for drinking, there are minimal chances of you failing. But if you start with the wrong breeds, wrong feeds, and wrong housing, you are setting yourself up for failure.

Today, it is no longer a secret that compared to other poultry birds, raising quails require less capital investment but offers great returns. As a result, this has stimulated commercial quail farming to gain fast popularity across the world. Did you know that with at least 50 birds, you can start commercial quail farming and within two to three years, start reaping millions from your investment? The trick is to consistently plough back all the profits into the quail farm for the first two to three years and thereafter, nothing can stop you from reaping the millions.

Profitable quail rearing requires that you carry out adequate research on what products you should be producing, and thereafter, make necessary plans to maximize on the production of those products. You can't profitably go wrong in quail farming if you focus on say, production of quail eggs or quail chicks and put your best foot forward.

Below are some of the products and byproducts linked to quail farming. The decision on which best product(s) you should settle on producing for profit at your farm is your personal call to make.

- **Unfertilized eggs:** When you raise female quails in isolation from male quails, the female quails will eventually lay unfertilized eggs once they reach the egg-laying stage. It is the absence of mating between mature male and mature female quails which result into laying of the unfertilized eggs by female quails.

   The production of unfertilized eggs is a common trend among a number of commercial quail farmers. You will find these eggs being sold in local supermarkets, groceries and even food outlets. These eggs are consumed daily by the masses across the globe since they can never hatch into quail chicks. Quail eggs are popularly referred to as "wonder eggs". They have been scientifically proven to contain enormous health and medicinal benefits, making them a favorite meal to a growing number of its consumers.

- **Fertilized eggs:** When you raise female quails in good proportion to male quails, they will lay fertilized eggs. Fertilized eggs are laid out of successful mating between male and female quails. These fertilized eggs have the potential to hatch into quail chicks.

  In order to guarantee fertility of the eggs, it is advisable to pair one male quail with two females. Or pair utmost one male to three females. That's the recommended ratio which may yield fertile quail eggs. Any pairing ratio beyond this is not guaranteed to yield fertilized eggs.

- **Quail chicks:** After successful completion of the incubation period, fertilized quail eggs would hatch into chicks. For commercial purposes, you need to focus on production of a few days old quail chicks since it is the most preferred age to acquire and start raising quails.

- **Point of lay quail birds:** These quails are between the ages of five to six weeks. They are at the stage of laying eggs. From hatching, you should take good care of quail chicks by feeding them on the right compositions of feeds and giving them relevant medications and fresh water. As a result, they will reach the point of lay in correct time and become productive thereafter, for a long period of time.

- **Manure:** Quails' wastes are a useful by-product for farming purposes. Quails' droppings are organic in nature with high levels of nitrogen. They are therefore, on high demand by many crop farmers world over.

- **Meat:** You can opt to raise broilers specifically for meat production, or have a mix up of both layers and broilers. Notably, when layers stop egg-laying, they become 'available' to be slaughtered for their meat. Quail's meat can be prepared and packed in frozen form for supply to local supermarkets and restaurants. You can smoke the meat on special orders for consumption. They have a nice taste and can stay preserved for a long period of time.

Why you don't need to purchase already egg-laying quails for commercial egg production

When female quails begin to lay eggs, it is never easy for an average quail farmer to tell their exact ages. It is therefore, possible to purchase quails in their second year of egg laying or possibly birds approaching their egg-laying-menopause if the purchase is made at the egg-laying stage.

Quail birds do slow down and would eventually stop putting on more weight as their approach full maturity. Therefore, just by looking at the size of any quail, at times it would not be easy to tell its exact age. It is equally proven through research, that female quail birds do lay eggs consistently within their first years of egg production. But in the subsequent years, their rate of egg production may slow down, or may become inconsistent and eventually, disappear as they age.

Did you know an egg laid by a four-year-old quail bird may be infertile? This may result into massive waste of resources by any farmer who purchases such birds in anticipation of incubating their eggs. .

If you intend to raise quails for commercial egg production, purchase utmost five weeks old quail birds. At that stage, their vitality and productiveness can be guaranteed. However, you have the capacity to hatch fertile quail eggs and successfully raise quail chicks, then that would be the most recommended option.

KEEPING QUAILS FOR FUN / AS A HOBBY

Within the aviary, it is recommended to keep quails together with doves, cockatiels, and budgerigars as quails will help clean up dropped feeds on the floor of the aviary.

If you intend to raise quails as a hobby or for the fun of it, an aviary would provide the best housing facility to use. Within the aviary, it is recommended to keep quails together with doves, cockatiels, and budgerigars as quails will easily clean up dropped feeds on the floor of the aviary. Equally, an aviary provides quails with enough headroom to fly up and minimize chances of banging their heads, unlike in cages where the headroom is limited and chances of banging their heads are high.

Quails prefer secluded areas such as corners, and like to nest on the floor/ground. They like hiding behind plants, trees and other greenery. Provide them with cut branches of trees such as conifer at the edges of the aviary. Equally, Quails do enjoy bathing in sand or soil. Therefore, mix wood chippings with either sand or soil and pour on the floor of the aviary, or put the mixture in some spacious box capable of allowing the birds to sand/soil-bathe.

A rabbit hutch or a small weld mesh run with an attached coop such as a broody coop used for housing a hen would equally be appropriate for housing two to four quail birds. But you must take precautionary measures when changing feeds or water since quails can easily escape from the run. Also remember to put wood shavings on the floor and provide the birds with sand or soil mixed with wood chippings/wood savings for dust-bathing.

Note: Sometimes mature males have a tendency to make some soft noise/sound. This should not scare you. Instead, it should guide you towards positioning the bird's house in a location where that sound/noise would not interfere with your peace, or your neighbor's.

HOUSING QUAILS

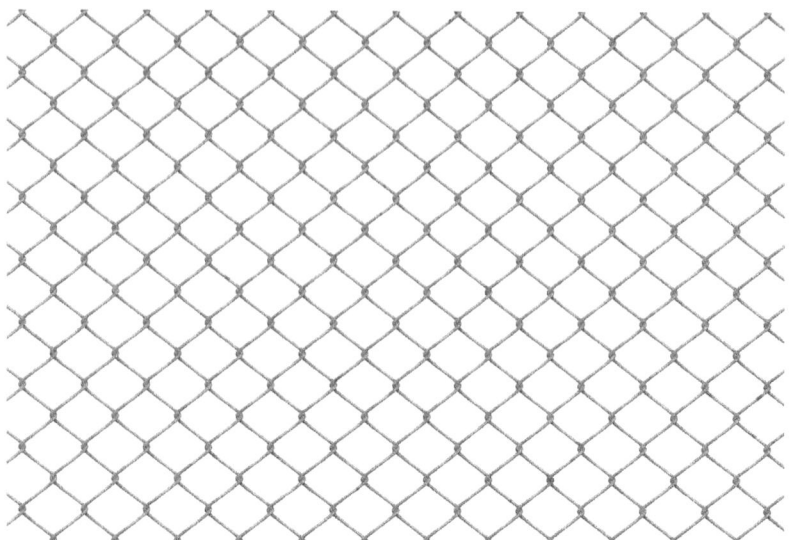

Quails start laying eggs at 6 weeks old and progress to attain 70% of egg production on the 8th week and onwards. Therefore, as they approach egg laying week, you should pair one male to two females, or one male to utmost three females. These are the most recommended ratios if you intend to get eggs which are 99.9% fertilized.

As already stated, if your desire is to raise quails for production of fresh eggs or meat for purposes of breeding or for profitable gains, raising them inside cages would be appropriate. But if your intention is to keep them for the fun of it/as a hobby, or as domestic pets, you can raise them in an aviary.

Use of cages

Use of cages is the most widely adopted method for raising domesticated quails, especial for commercial purposes. The cages are specially built using wood and wire mesh with spaces of 2sq ft per bird.

It is recommended to construct the floor of the cages with a wire mesh capable of letting the birds' droppings to fall on the ground with ease. The wire mesh too should have the capacity to bar predators. ¼ inch of wire mesh would be best ideal to use in constructing the floor of the cages, however, in most instances, it doesn't effectively permit quails' dropping to pass through. Therefore, ½ inch of wire mesh would be appropriate. But as you settle on using ½ inch of wire mesh, you must consider the birds' predators which might be lurking in the area. A good way to bar the predators is by raising the cages from the ground or putting metal barriers on the stands of the cages.

There are two ways of acquiring quail cages:
- You can purchase already built cages from local quail-cage dealers or quail breeders.
- You can construct one.

Considerably, when raising quails inside a cage, ensure the cages are spacious enough to give the birds some freedom of moving or turning around. This is vital to help prevent stressing the birds. Stressed quail birds are usually unproductive!

Use of a coop/pen house

Here, quails are kept in a typical house-like structure and provided with feeds, drinking water, a source of heat (for the chicks) and protection from predators. However, most people prefer to keep quails outdoors due to an ammonium-like smell emitted from their droppings.

Consider spreading wood shavings or saw dust on the floor of the pen. They will aid absorbing the birds' droppings to form dry crumbs which are easy to clean out of the coop.

In case you have any un-utilized structure in the farm, say like some shed or even a barn, you can convert it into a coop by covering it with recommended wire mesh to protect the birds from predators and to also bar the birds from escaping away.

Use of an aviary

As stated earlier, if you are raising quails for the fun of it, or as a hobby, an aviary would provide the best housing facility to use. An aviary is an enclosure with adequate room for the housed birds to easily fly around.

Within the aviary, it is recommended to keep quails together with doves, cockatiels and budgerigars. Quail breeds like the Chinese painted quails are good *aviary cleaners*. They feed on the feeds spilled on the floor of aviaries by other birds. This helps in curbing feed wastage and keeps the aviary clean from feed spillage.

However, since quails have a unique personality, raising them in an aviary may result into lower egg production. It is therefore not recommended to raise quails in an aviary for commercial egg production. Also, due to the open nature of most aviaries, quails may be exposed to occasional extreme temperatures. Too hot or too cold temperatures may have adverse effects on the birds' health and thus, negatively affect their production.

Note: In case you want to let the quails to roam freely in any open field, you should first clip their wings to prevent them from hopping away. Many people have lost their quail birds due to releasing them in the open field without proper clipping of the birds' wings.

FEEDING QUAILS
From quail chicks to adult quails

The more you feed quails on different feeds, the more you will learn about their favorite feeds. For quality output from the birds, you need to feed them on nutritious and well balanced feeds.

For your quail farming to remain a profitable venture, the birds must be well fed on nutritious and well-balanced feeds. Due to their smaller body sizes, quails are adapted to consuming fewer amounts of feeds on a daily basis. One interesting fact with the feeding habits of quail birds is that they usually eat as much as they should. Therefore, you should never have any worry on any risk of overfeeding them. They know when to stop.

Quails need the feeds to help them stay active and productive throughout their lifespan. Well balanced feeds usually assist their bodies to develop immunity against diseases.

In case you buy quail chicks from a breeder or a quail farmer who doesn't take good care of the birds, ensure you feed the chicks on electrolytes and some warm water mixed with vitamins.

Here is a detailed simple guide on feeding quails, from quail chicks to adult quails.

Starter Feeds: Immediately quail chicks are hatched, start them off with "chick starter". Chick starters are usually rich in proteins which the quail chicks are in need of at that development stage. Feed them on the starter feeds until they are 3-4 weeks old.

The protein content within the starter feeds usually varies depending on the type of quail chicks you are keeping. The starter feeds for layers normally has higher levels of protein when compared with the starter feeds for males.

You need to liaise with nearby experienced quail farmers/breeders or poultry vets for recommendations on the best starter feeds that will best suit your quail breeds. As a good recommendation, you can feed them on game bird feeds /turkey feeds (a starter feed with an average protein component of 25%).

Regular Feeds: Past four, five or six weeks old (depending on the recommendations from the experienced quail farmer/breeder or poultry vet), you should graduate the starter feeds to regular feeds. Even at that stage, the feeds should still be constituted with a good percentage of proteins.

There are different regular feeds, or what others refer to as growers mash, for male quails (broilers) and for female quails (hens). Ensure you get a good recommendation for the right growers mash from experienced quail bird farmers /breeders/ poultry vets.

Other invaluable tips on feeding quails

Did you know quails can comfortably consume commercial chicken feeds? However, you need to increase protein contents of the commercial chicken feeds to be compatible with the high protein levels demanded by quail birds. Equally, since quails are known fussy eaters, you should buy quail pellets in mini sacks of say 25kgs each (in case you have a few pairs of quails), as the feeds may go off before your quails feed on all of it

Non-medicated game bird feed is invaluably ideal to give to the birds as it rich in proteins. And in the absence of commercial feeds, the birds can feed on soya meals, groundnut cakes, fish meals, sorghum, sunflower cakes, maize seeds (corn seeds), deoiled rice bran etc. In addition to provision of quality feeds, do not forget to give the birds clean and fresh water. Equally, give them grit to help them improve on their digestion of consumed feeds.

You can supplement their diet with kitchen scraps such as sweet corn, grated carrot, and broccoli, chunks of apple, lettuce, cut cabbages and even peas. You can also feed them on millet or mealworms. Notably, mature male quails usually shy from eating mealworms. Instead, they present the mealworms to the hens as a sign of appreciation.

Note: The more you feed quails on different feeds, the more you will learn about their favorite feeds. However, desist from feeding them on fresh cuttings from the garden as it is easy to mix in a poisonous plant. Equally, never feed them on avocado or chocolate since the two are poisonous to a number of birds.

QUAIL DISEASES

The four most common quail diseases, preventions and treatments

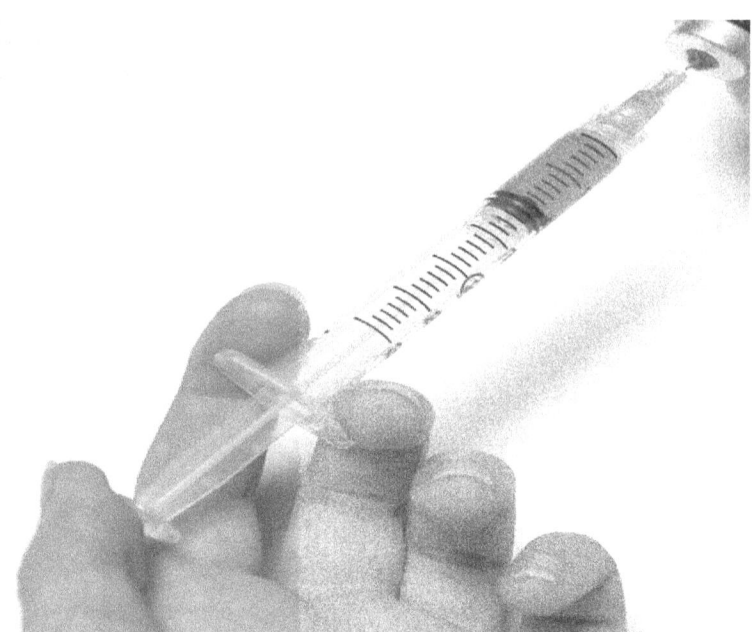

Quails are hardy birds known to be resistant to a number of diseases affecting poultry birds.

An average quail farmer may not clearly identify and offer an effective diagnosis and treatments to quail diseases at the farm level without relevant training, experience and equipments. Specifically, without training and proper equipments, it would be difficult to diagnose internal infections.

Quails are hardy birds known to be resistant to a number of diseases affecting poultry birds. Interestingly, lots of research on diseases affecting quails is ongoing and hopefully, future quail bird farmers will have a broader knowledge on dealing with the most common and emerging quail diseases.

Below are the four most common quail diseases, preventions and treatments.

- **Coccidiosis:** Coccidiosis is a parasitic infection which has a severe effect on the digestive tracts of quail birds. It normally attacks quails which are less than 7 weeks. (Quail birds beyond 7 weeks of age are usually resistant to Coccidiosis, but in cases where they are attacked by the disease, the impact is usually not as severe as it is to birds below 7 weeks of age).

Since Coccidiosis affects the digestive tract of the birds, the infected birds would generally slow down and eventually stop feeding. They will subsequently grow weak, pale and weak legged. If not attended to on time, the infected birds may die.

Prevention and Treatment: Universally, Coccidiosis affects quails and other poultry birds out of poor management of farms i.e. failure to keep the poultry houses clean and dry. Coccidiosis mainly thrive where there is a buildup of wet quail droppings and in moist areas around water points and feeders. Therefore, you need to ensure the cages are dry and free of wet quail droppings. Usually, it is advisable to construct areas around feeders and water points using wire mesh. This ensures no quail dropping accumulates within the cages.

Certain quail feeds are laced with coccidiostat; a drug that helps prevents infection by Coccidiosis. To the birds which are not yet infected with Coccidiosis, the consumption of coccidiostat in the feeds allows them limited infection with Coccidiosis, and thereafter, they develop immunity against the disease.

- **Worms (Capillary Worms/Thread Worms/Crop Worms):** The second disease or rather parasite which affects quails is worms. Specifically, the most dangerous of the worms are those that infect the lining of the birds' crop(s). Capillary worms, scientifically known as *Capillaria spp.* falls in this category. The infection caused by capillary worms can never be diagnosed by merely looking at the bird physically. It's only when the crop of an infected bird is removed, or when the crop of a bird which has died of the infection is removed and opened, and then worms which appear thread-like can be seen lining across the tissue fragments of the bird's crop.

The infected birds often eat a lot but always appear as if they are starving. And in the last stages of infection, the infected birds often experience difficulty in breathing. These are the two most common physical symptoms of a bird infected with capillary worms.

Prevention and Treatment: Capillary worms usually thrive in wet droppings and on wet areas around feeders and waterers. The best way to control infection and spread of capillary worms is by constructing the base of the birds' cages with wire mesh. Spaces on the wire mesh would not allow build-up of quails' wet droppings and thus, will prevent the birds from picking the disease from the cages and lessen its spread if any. (The cages should be raised from the ground).

To treat capillary worms, it is recommended you use a correct wormer (de-wormer). Consult experienced poultry vets within your area for recommendations on an appropriate wormer (de-wormer), since the names of these drugs differ from one country to another.

- **Histomoniasis:** This is one of the most lethal diseases affecting quail birds. Histomoniasis is also known as the blackhead. It is a protozoan infection which attacks a number of poultry breeds. In fact, it is usually referred to as a disease of the larger fowl unit.

Histomoniasis infects the liver of quail birds and immediately, starts to produce necrotic lesions which eventually results into fatal liver damages of the infected birds. The infected birds often exhibit restlessness, poor appetite, loss of feathers and sulfur-like-colored droppings.

Prevention and Treatment: It is believed chickens which have recovered from histomoniasis are its carrier. Therefore, as a precautionary measure, avoid mixing chickens with quail birds under the same housing.

For treatment purposes, you should use relevant wormers (de-wormers), to help eliminate cecal worms which transmit histomoniasis. However, the most effective treatment for histomoniasis lies in its prevention. No effective medication has been approved for its treatment (at the time of writing this book).

- **Ulcerative Enteritis:** Ulcerative enteritis is another destructive quail bird disease. From its name, the disease occurs like an ulcer on the internal linings of the infected birds' intestines. However, the most effective way to diagnose Ulcerative enteritis is through laboratory analysis.

The disease can easily be transmitted from one infected bird to the other through contact with the droppings of the infected bird. It has too been established that birds which have recovered from ulcerative enteritis are usually its carriers.

Prevention and Treatment: The most effective ways to prevent spread of this fatal disease lies in exercising clean sanitary measures and in the quick identification and quarantine of the infected birds. It is also recommended that you should clean up the cages off any wet droppings, and it is essential the holding areas of the cages be built with wire mesh to help stop any accumulation of the birds' wet droppings.

For treatment, you need to liaise with your local experienced poultry vet for recommendations on effective drugs to use.

Signs exhibited by sick quails.

Just like other breeds of poultry, sick quails will tend to exhibit some of the below characteristics:

- **Numb, un-alert and unresponsive**: Sick quails usually appear numb and un-alert. They are unresponsive to any touch, and will mostly be seen sleeping on the floor of their housing. But if standing, they will tend to exhibit an abnormal posture.

- **Reduction in productivity**: If there is a sudden reduction in the number of eggs laid by hens, that could be a sign of disease infection with the flock.

- **Very high or very low body temperatures**: You should occasionally check the body temperatures of quails to establish if any could be exhibiting very high or very low temperatures. Such could be a sign of disease infection.

- **Lack of appetite**: Sick quails lack normal appetite and as a result, consume lesser quantities of feeds compared to the quantities of feeds they do normally feed on.

- **Weight loss**: Due to lack of appetite, a sick quail may register weight loss and begin to appear weak, dehydrated and pale-faced.

- **Lackluster behavior**: Sick quails may appear gloomy, and are usually disinterested even when you give them feeds or water.

- **Observable defects in defecations**: When the defecation appears bloodstained, that's a sure sign of internal infection. If it has an accompaniment of worms, that's a sign of parasitic infection. If it is very hard, or very watery, those could be signs of dehydration, and diarrhea, respectively.

- **Difficulty in breathing**: Blocked mucus membranes, or any observable or hearable sound indicating some difficulty in breathing by any bird is a sign of a respiratory disease infection; possibly pneumonia.

- **Plumage**: If the feathers are falling off, or appear rough in texture, be sure to closely check the affected bird for possible disease infection.

The least thing you should do when you identify a sick bird is to isolate it with speed from the rest of the flock. Afterwards, you should seek for the services of a poultry vet to help you effectively diagnose and possibly treat the affected bird.

Note: Always desist from trying to offer treatments on your own to any sick quail if you aren't sure about the disease it is suffering from.

Factors making quails to be susceptible to disease or pest infections.

Below are some of the leading factors making quails to be susceptible to disease infections.

- **Age:** Did you know that older quails are usually prone to disease infections? This is due to their weakened body defense mechanisms. Equally, younger quails are too, prone to infection by certain diseases due to their not-fully developed body immune system.

- **Physical injuries:** Any physical injury on any part of a quail's body may make it susceptible to bacterial infections. Such injuries may be caused by other quails, quail's owner, or even by the affected quail.

- **Environment:** Very cold or very chilly weather conditions may make it possible for quails to contract respiratory diseases like pneumonia.

- **Sex of quail birds:** Did you know that due to their frequency in laying eggs, hens are more prone to disease infections as compared to roosters?

- **Poor sanitation:** Unhygienic housing conditions may spur an outbreak of certain contagious diseases like Coccidiosis.

- **Mixing of other poultry breeds with quails:** This too may easily facilitate spread of contagious diseases within your flock. If you mix quails and chickens in the same housing, any chicken suffering from a disease like say histomoniasis may easily transmit it to quails.

Effective ways of dealing with quail pests and diseases

Below are some of the ways to help you deal with a number of quail pests and diseases

- Always raise the birds under sanitary conditions. The moment you choose to raise your birds negligently, under unsanitary conditions, be rest assured that even the best of quail drugs when administered, will always be rendered ineffective. Raising quails under sanitary conditions is your first step towards raising healthy birds.

- Ensure the quails' house is always clean and properly disinfected. Wet and uncollected quails' droppings around water points and feeding zones may expose the birds to some deadly infections like Coccidiosis.

- Dust the birds with appropriate pesticides in order to keep external parasites away.

- Their house should be well constructed to shield the birds from wind, hot sun, rodents like snakes, and other domestic pets like cats and dogs.

- Construct their house with cold insulators to keep the house warm during winter, and provide enough ventilation to cool down their house during hot summer. Equally, the house should have adequate exposure to light (natural or artificial).

- Always feed your flock on quality and well-balanced diet. You need to purchase quail feeds and other feed supplements which contain the right amounts of nutrients needed by the birds. If done right, you should expect quality eggs/meat from your flock, coupled with hardy birds resistant to a number of diseases.

- Give quails clean and fresh water for drinking, placed at strategic positions where they do not need any unnecessary strain to access to it. It is usually advisable to give them water at room temperature. Avoid giving them very cold or very hot water as they will avoid drinking such.

- When some quails begin to physically appear weak or gloomy, isolate them from the rest of the flock, as fast as you can, and closely observe them for any possible illness.

- De-worm the birds regularly using recommended de-wormers. This will aid in preventing infestations by worms and other protozoan diseases.

- De-beak any noted cannibal with the flock to bar them from inflicting wounds on other birds, which may subsequently make the wounded birds be susceptible to bacterial infections.

STRESS AND VICES IN QUAILS
Causes and Preventative Measures

You should identify and cull with speed, any bird with noted pecking disorder. Possibly, you can de-beak such birds. The tendency to peck other birds is commonly exercised by male birds. If not checked, they can end up blinding other birds and in extreme cases, the affected birds may end up dying.

Stress is any condition imposed on the birds making them to be uncomfortable. Stress causes disturbance to the birds and prevents them from eating well. Equally, it prevents female quails from laying well.

Below are some of the most common causes of stress in quails:

- Sudden extreme temperatures (very hot and very cold temperatures).
- Sudden change in the daily routine, i.e. sudden change in type of feeds, sudden change in feed locations, sudden change in locations of waterers, etc.

- Sudden loud noises like thunderstorms, loud music, noisy automobiles, low flying aero planes, etc.
- Insufficient or lack of enough feeds and water.
- Presence of strangers, pests, and predators.
- Introduction of new birds in the old flock.
- Improper handling of the birds during culling or during vaccination.
- Overcrowding in the quails' house, forcing the birds to compete for space, feeds and water.

Dealing with stress in quails

Below are some practices which you can adopt to help you manage stress in quails:

- If you must change any daily routine, do it gradually.
- Effectively, control any diseases or parasites affecting the birds.
- Insulate their house appropriately to guarantee uniform temperatures throughout the year.
- Shield the quails from loud noise.
- Gradually, introduce new birds to the flock.
- Minimize access to the poultry house by strangers.
- Keep the correct number of birds per housing unit and provide each housing unit with adequate balanced feeds and waterers.
- Handle the birds carefully during culling or during vaccination.

Vices in quails

Vices are bad habits that quails develop due to their environmental exposure. The two most common quail vices are egg eating, and cannibalism.

Below are some of the factors which may expose quails to develop vices.

- Idleness. An idle quail can easily turn destructive!
- Broken or soft-shelled eggs may tempt most quails to want to peck such eggs.
- Any delay in collection of laid eggs may tempt the hens to peck the eggs.
- Lack of minerals such as calcium and phosphorus in the feeds may force the birds to peck elsewhere in their pursuit.
- Overcrowding in the quails' house may force a number of hens to lay eggs on areas where other birds can easily access them and possibly try to peck them.
- Still, overcrowding may encourage some quails to peck one another; possibly, in hope of removing external pests from one another.
- Introduction of new birds with bad habits into an old flock with no bad habits may tempt the old birds to pick up such new bad habits from the new birds.
- Mixing birds of different age groups may expose birds of younger age to bullying by birds of older age.
- In case they are laying eggs is a nesting box, presence of a bright light in the laying nests, may expose the laid eggs to pecking by female birds.
- Female quails with disorders. Immediately a female quail lays an egg and then starts to move around even before

its cloaca retracts, this might excite other birds to want to peck it.

Controlling vices in quails

Below are some precautionary measures you can take to help you control vices in quails:

- Keep the birds busy by supplying them with green vegetables, hanged appropriately within their house. The vegetables or greens should be free from sprays of pesticides.
- Keep the light around or within the laying boxes at minimum to block the hens from seeing the laid eggs.
- Collect eggs frequently from the nests. Two to three times in a day.
- Cull and debeak any noted cannibal within the flock.
- Cull hens which exhibit prolapse. Those whose cloaca takes time to retract. This will stop tempting other birds from pecking affected birds.
- Provide the birds with well-balanced and nutritious feeds, containing all the necessary nutrients and minerals they need.
- Keep the birds according to their age groups to thwart bullying of younger birds by birds of older ages.
- Keep the correct number of birds per housing unit, with adequate balanced feeds and waterers provided.
- Dust the birds regularly to effectively contain external parasites.

It is proverbially connoted that prevention is better than cure. Once quails are infected by any disease, below are the possible outcomes: Losing them to the disease. Or incurring costly expenses on their treatments.

RAISING HEALTHY QUAILS

When your quails are well fed, disease-free and happy, they will reward you with lots of quality eggs for an extended period of time, and provide you with a delicious and nutritious meat throughout your quail farming years.

A quail bird is regarded to be in a state of good health when all its body organs and systems are normal and functioning well. Here below are the seven reasons why it is important to keep healthy quails:

- Need for quality eggs and meat. I am sure you would not be happy to see your quails lay eggs which have attachments of any parasitic larvae. You want to see them laying clean and fresh eggs. Equally, I am sure you would not appreciate non-delicious quail meat, or meat obtained from sick birds. You want delicious quail meat obtained from healthy and disease-free birds.

- Healthy quails have inability to spread any contagious diseases among themselves, and, or to human beings.

- Healthy quails are vibrant, mature fast and have a longer lifespan. They are generally associated with high productivity.

- Healthy quails are cost-effective to raise. You will have very minimal bills related to their treatments.

- Unlike sick quails, healthy quails have a higher market value. They fetch higher prices.

Below are the basic essentials to help you raise healthy quails

- Be in possession of relevant and up-to-date information on raising quails. Know what you are getting into and how best you will effectively stay in it. It's that simple! Have enough and relevant information on the latest developments in the quail farming industry, plus relevant latest general market trends in the poultry farming industry.

- Have the right quail breeds from the word go, depending on your purpose for keeping the birds. Aim to adhere to the age-old breeding rule: *If you start with a desirable breed, you should expect a desirable output. But if you start with an undesirable breed, you should expect an undesirable output.*

- Have the correct housing facility or space for quails to be safely reared, depending on your choice for keeping the birds: in cages, in an aviary or in pens.

- Have the correct information and knowledge on quail feeds and basic disease management practices. In case you may be disadvantaged with such information or such knowledge, readily seek for the services of experienced quail or poultry professionals within your area.

- Occasionally, expose the birds to sunlight. They need that precious sunlight's vitamin D.

- Provide them with enough and well-balanced feeds, clean and fresh water for drinking (at room temperature).

- Provide the birds with grit to aid in food digestion.

- Supply them with greens (vegetables) to supplement their feeds. You can hang these vegetables in their house/cage to keep them busy as they continually peck them.

- Good grooming and good sanitation. You must effectively take care of the birds under a clean environment. This can never be overstated. Equally, you need to handle the birds properly during culling or during vaccination.

- To help contain spread of diseases, it is advisable to disinfect the birds, the cages, the waterers, and the feeders correctly with recommended disinfectors. External parasites such as ticks, lice, and mice may attack the birds under unsanitary conditions and infect them with fatal diseases such as histomoniasis (histomonosis).

- Peaceful environment. Just like other poultry breeds, quails too detest noisy surroundings. They will remain unproductive in noisy setups.

In a nutshell, when your quails are well fed, disease-free and happy, they will reward you with quality eggs for an extended period of time, and provide you with delicious and nutritious meat throughout your quail farming years. The key to a fulfilling quail farming adventure is to aim to raise healthy quail birds. You will never regret raising healthy quail birds.

www.ingramcontent.com/pod-product-compliance
Lightning Source LLC
Chambersburg PA
CBHW060417190526
45169CB00002B/944